Beyond All Odds
A Story of Faith, Courage, and the Realities of War

A World War II Memoir By

Donald F. Vonachen

Copyright © 1994, 2015 by the Donald Vonachen Family,
Peoria, Illinois

All rights reserved.

ISBN: 1514770202
ISBN-13: 978-1514770207

CONTENTS

Foreword   i

Beyond All Odds   1

Epilogue   58

FOREWORD

My grandfather finished this memoir June 21, 1994. Until creating this semi-professional version in the summer of 2015 it had only survived as unbound copies of a copy, which had been distributed amongst his children and their families. His work has been converted to a digital format for posterity, and so that it can be easily published in this book you are now holding.

All attempts have been made to preserve the format and character of the original document. While editing I uncovered some grammatical errors and inconsistencies, most of which I chose not to fix to maintain Bud's voice, style, and original intent.

For example, the name of the village where he was originally stationed is spelled three different ways in the original text: Lommersweimer, Lommesweimer, and Lommensweimer. Since I have been unable to locate this village and its proper spelling, they have been left as they were originally written.

Some insignificant spelling errors have also been corrected, but otherwise the text remains as it was originally written 21 years ago.

Chris Ellbogen

BEYOND ALL ODDS

At approximately 5:30 a.m. on Saturday, December 16, 1944 the Germans launched a last ditch offensive in Belgium and Luxembourg. This offensive has come to be known as the "Battle of the Bulge." The equivalent of over twenty-five German Divisions, including ten armored Divisions, pushed off an offensive which was intended to split the allied forces and move to the sea.

The ensuing battle which took place was a do or die, kill or be killed confrontation, termed by many as the most vicious and bloody battle of the European Front in World War II. This battle had everything a military strategist could imagine, including but not limited to surprise, unbelievable adverse odds, freezing weather, and a dramatic resolution which greatly affected the ultimate outcome of World War II.

From dawn on December 16, 1944 until dusk of December 22, 1944 the 106th greatly outnumbered

Division, very young and very green, stood in the way of Hitler's ultimate goal. By dusk on December 22, 1944 the 106th (Golden Lion Division) was destroyed.

Out of 16,000 approximate souls in this Division, 10,000 to 12,000 were killed, wounded or captured in that short period of time.

The Battle of the Bulge is mostly noted for the heroic defense of Bastogne, Belgium to the South by the 101st airborne division. The 106th Division is mostly known for the loss of more men in infantry combat in a shorter period of time than perhaps had occurred in United States Military history.

Actually, the Battle of the Bulge occurred between two anchor points. The anchor line to the North was St. Vith. The anchor to the South was Bastogne. Between these two areas the Germans made a devastating bulge in the allied lines. Without taking anything away from what history has recorded or the credit given those at Bastogne for their gallantry, the real story of the bulge may well have taken place in and about the area of St. Vith. It revolved about not the 12,000 dead, wounded or prisoner from the 106th Division, but the remnants of that Division who, along with several other Divisions with little direction subsequently held the line and blunted the Northern attack of the German Army. The drama and the story involves not only young and untried troops but the fact that the entire allied command was in a complete state of confusion, on line many of the troops were virtually leaderless, and all supplies and food had been taken away or were lost in the Paris black market. The troops had no warm clothing, the winter was the most severe in 20th century Europe. The entire scene was one of complete chaos.

Against these unbelievable odds history was turned around at St. Vith. The mammoth counter offensive of Adolph Hitler was completely stalled.

This account is the personal story of one man's date with destiny.

I was a member of B Company, 424th Regiment, of the 106th Infantry Division. On December 16, 1944 our Regiment was located in a very small village called Lommersweimer, in Belgium or Luxembourg. Several days prior the 422nd and 423rd regiments of our division had moved into the battle line replacing the 2nd Infantry Division which was being sent back for rest and rehabilitation. Company B was in reserve, i.e. a backup position.

We had landed at LeHavre only several days before and moved by truck to billets in the little village. If you would attempt to find Lommersweimer on a map you would not be successful unless your plat was very detailed. I do not know if it exists today.

At LeHavre we had been congratulated and assured that we had received a "plum" for our first battle assignment. This was a very static area, both sides were solidly entrenched and because of the rough and almost impenetrable terrain impasse had existed for a considerable period of time. Battle activities had long been confined to holding positions. This was not an area where you were going to get the fluid flow of battle or resulting high casualties. We were apprehensive, but assured that perhaps our chances of survival were much greater in this position than almost any other along the Western front. Activity consisted of very minor artillery action from time to time and also some intermittent patrol activity, which allowed each side insight on the strength and/or intentions of the other. The battle line was some miles from Lommesweimer on a plain called Schnee Eifel on the edge of the Ardennes forest and near the Siegfried line. The biggest and only significant town in the locale was St. Vith.

The 106th although young and green consisted to a great extent of young men of high IQ's who had been involved in army educational programs, now discontinued. There were a few retreads and the division had been filled in with recruits many of whom were not properly trained for battle.

Personally I was as prepared for this sort of thing as I ever could be, both physically and emotionally. While not looking forward to the risks involved, I was rather excited about the pending adventure. However the thought of using a gun or killing someone appalled me. When the time came would I be able to pull a trigger? It occurred to me that I probably was not as adult or as tough as I tried to act.

I was a PFC and had just turned 19 years of age. I recall our leaving England in the dead of night and traveling a consistently changing course across the English Channel. This was pretty much the pattern of troop transfer in those days and the continual direction changes were to avoid German submarines.

One evening on the boat our Squad Lieutenant called a number of us in to discuss the war. He opened and passed around a bottle of whiskey. We calculated prospects as we took turns sipping. He dwelt on the fact that we were such "nice boys" and it rather disturbed him after polling, that none had even done battle in the streets, been involved in gang wars, or violence. I recalled responding that we would be brave and outgoing soldiers; one didn't have to go around spending his life with a knife or with guns in order to do what had to be done in a moment of crisis. Needless to say I thought of those words of bravado many times later. How easy it is to be tough before the actual test.

The landing operation at LeHavre had been kept quite secret. Under the cover of night we climbed down the side of our ship which had stopped out at the edge of the harbor and slid down nets which were strung along the entire port side. We then jumped from the nets to small landing craft which carried us to the beach. Arrival day was very windy. There were high waves. Since we had to carry all our personal, heavy equipment and rifle on our backs the maneuvering to the landing craft was somewhat precarious. We were informed several lost their lives when they slipped and/or missed the boat.

The horrible evidence of D-Day was about us as we approached the shore. Hulls of upended ships emerged vertically from the water. Destroyed tanks and other vehicles appeared along the shore. Many of them hovered grotesquely in the shallow waters of the immediate beach.

Our landing craft hit the beach. We waded ashore. It was raining quite hard. We were immediately herded to an area of assembly for troops to be deployed for transportation to the front. It had been storming for quite a time. We were standing ankle deep in mud, but spent the entire night where we were and were ordered to pitch tents in the mud. This was the beginning of many stupid decisions which plagued us as we went in to battle. I can't describe my disgust. It was a mess.

That particular night I came upon communication men on the beach. They were huddled around a radio, having just set up their equipment. They allowed me into their tent and we listened to "Axis Sally," a turncoat American woman who had become a Nazi commentator. Sally broadcast in English. She was describing in detail the deployment and landing of the 106th Infantry Division, including all division final plans and where we were to be fighting. She described how we would be spread out and even the positions we would hold. From time to time she would interrupt her discourse to play nostalgic American music interspersed with comments about the girls and wives left at home enjoying the Christmas Season, without a thought of us, and of course with new boyfriends.

We laughed, but I must admit it was a bit disconcerting as we realized that the Germans were aware of our every move; where we had sailed from, where we were going and what our plans were. Sally had more information than our immediate superiors.

The next morning a Chaplain said Mass and gave Communion from the hood of a truck. He gave us general absolution, and speculated that for some of us, this could be our last time on earth to receive the Blessed Sacrament; that perhaps many of us would not return. Little did he realize the truth of those words.

We were quickly piled into trucks and crossed France, Belgium and Luxembourg to our destination Lommensweimer. We were specifically commanded to neatly keep our neck ties in place. On arriving we encountered the members of the 2nd Division, moving out. They were dirty, caked with mud and caricatures of the usually accepted version of front line G.I.'s. Their hoots and calls about the ties were embarrassing.

We spent a day or two at the billet before the Battle of the Bulge began. During that idle time, some of us decided to "shut up" a big mouth.

He was a young man from the Bronx, totally obnoxious with twangy New York accent, an expert on "everything." The night before the Battle of the Bulge started, we made up our minds that we had had enough of his bullshit. To him we were hicks from the boondocks. He put down all "inferior" Midwestern counterparts. We resorted to the "snipe hunt."

I explained to him that we were in the snipe hunting capital of the world; that this presented an opportunity which we could little afford to overlook. He was taken aback and admitted he didn't understand what "snipe" were. We assured him it was a very harmless little animal and absolutely magnificent to the taste. If he was interested in attempting to capture snipe we made it clear this would be the time and place to do so; and also this would be an experience to tell to his grandchildren, perhaps the chance of a lifetime.

He was given very detailed instructions on how to capture snipe. I recalled the only way they possibly could be caught was in a paper bag and that you had to wear gloves as any scent of human hands would keep the snipe away. It was necessary to wave a flashlight in a backward "Z" motion in order to attract its attention; that the snipe would then run directly into the bag and thus you would capture them. We then sat down to decide who among us should go because if there was more than one, the snipe would become frightened and run. More instructions were detailed. By strange fate we drew straws and our friend from the East won as our designated representative. There was a considerable area of cleared farm land in front of the billets where we were staying. In the middle of that area was a small wooded glen. Our enemy who we hadn't yet heard from were apparently located on the other side of these woods. We decided that that little woods would be the place for him to go. So with gloves on, several sacks and a flashlight he took off on the hunt. By this time he was not so keen about the adventure. We made it clear that if he didn't have the courage to grab this opportunity there would be one or more of us who would be delighted to be the group representative. It was with some disbelief that we watched him swallow the bait. We embellished "ad nauseam" on the hunting procedures.

He entered the little wooded area approximately one hundred yards away, and we followed the light from his zig-zagging flashlight as he roamed through the woods. All of a sudden there was a barrage of artillery from the other side. Shells began landing in the wooded area. The Germans had also seen the flashing light.

The next time I saw him he was in the hands of an irate Sergeant who was demanding to know what the hell he was doing, and what had happened to his rifle and helmet. He had dropped those (a cardinal sin for any foot soldier) and taken off out of the woods as fast as he could go. His face and hands were badly scratched plowing through the underbrush. He was terrified. We had for all time silenced the big mouth, or so I thought.

Later I asked him how the snipe hunt went before the barrage.

He replied: "I had three of them in the bag and was ready to bring them home before those bastards starting shooting at me."

I surrendered. There was no question that he was always going to have the last word. We speculated later that these may well have been the first shots fired in the Battle of the Bulge. Can you imagine what must have gone through the German Commander's mind as they secretly were lining up tanks, artillery and troops -- and a zig-zag light appeared only a few hundred yards away from their position?

The story emphasizes that we really hadn't yet grown up. It didn't take long for that to happen. In retrospect one had to consider the stupidity of this ploy and potential resulting tragedy the snipe hunt could have created. We were wild, undisciplined and not very effective soldiers.

On the afternoon of December 16th or 17th (I can't recall which) we were called together. The 422nd and 423rd regiments were in deep trouble and had been surrounded by masses of attacking German troops. We were called up from reserve to reinforce our other two regiments.

We were ordered to store our duffel bags in trucks which were available and prepare for battle wearing only light jackets and, of course, our military gear. We had to be quite mobile, able to move very quickly. At this point three factors come to mind which had great impact on the lives of each of us: 1) allied intelligence had no knowledge of the buildup of the Nazi troops nor did they understand that the finest of the SS troops and armored divisions had been pulled from the Eastern front before this big battle; 2) our division had been strung out over an extremely large sector (over 27 miles) instead of the usual distance allowed for an infantry division. This allowed tremendous gaps and resulted in lack of communication between our units, and limited our effectiveness; 3) the decision to not take overcoats, blankets and other warm equipment was a disastrous one. The winter was to turn out to be the coldest and most fierce in the history of modern Europe. Without blankets or even coats this resulted in a suffering and loss of limbs for many. No American troops could have suffered more from the elements on a continuing basis than those who fought in this battle.

We climbed aboard waiting trucks and were driven toward the front. After traveling for some miles we came to an isolated crossroads and the trucks stopped. A higher ranking officer came by and talked to the Sergeant.

It was necessary to have someone man this road because it was a critical junction approaching the battle sector. He asked for the automatic riflemen of the squad. That happened to be me. I was directed to leave the squad and alone take up a position in a pillbox at this road junction. My instructions were clear. No one was to pass under any circumstances unless I knew who they were or who gave me the password of the day. Under no circumstances was I to allow any unknown person to pass or to enter into this area. Quickly, they re-mounted the trucks and sped off leaving me alone at this desolate intersection. The prospect of confronting unknown forces alone was frightening.

     I was at this spot for several hours. No one bothered me except persons from our company or other known members of the division. I can recall taking my hunting knife from its case and sticking it in the side of the pillbox so that I would readily have it available, if necessary. I had a good number of hours to think and had made up my mind under no conditions would I possibly allow myself to be taken prisoner. It was obvious, of course, that with a force of any size coming into the area I was a sitting duck and would either have to fight my way out or be captured. Fortunately for me the problem was not a real one.

     Unbelievable overhead artillery barrages from the front created constant explosions in the distance. Not to know what was happening and not to be a part of what my friends were going through was very disconcerting. From time to time, truck drivers would pull up, stop and talk to me, giving full accounts of what was going on in the front. Our company was being literally massacred by a numerically superior enemy.

One driver who was a little guy, highly excitable, explained the carnage by giving names and in detail terrible things that had happened to some of my friends. One of his comments was "this artillery is terrible; they're running around up there without any arms or legs." As I thought about this later, it seemed that he might have overdramatized the situation a little bit. He was correct in one detail, however. Our entire division was being destroyed. He left to carry a message to his commanding officer indicating he would be back in a few minutes. That was the last time I saw him. I can recall thinking of the terrible happenings and being alone. My imagination ran wild. I prayed for all my friends and also that I would be able to honorably do what was necessary when the time came. It was pretty obvious that my time was running out also, and somehow being alone and not involved seemed worse than actually being part of the battle.

Shortly thereafter a number of trucks came by with large remnants of the division, most of whom were not known to me. The man in charge who I think was a Colonel gathered a number of us together, maybe 100 or more, and told us our troops had been surrounded and were being cut to pieces by the Germans. We had to retreat. However, we couldn't retreat unless we fought our way out. He asked for volunteers to go forward to front positions to delay the enemy. He made it clear no one would be compelled to do this. For all practical purposes it appeared to be possibly a suicidal mission. I volunteered as did a number of others. We were sent forward to delay the Germans while hopefully our troops could retreat and regroup to come back at a later time.

My volunteering was an act of almost guilt at not having been with my friends in their hour of need. I don't know why I felt guilty, because I had been doing what I was directed to do, but I very strongly needed to be part of the group who would try to allow those remaining to escape. We were shipped to the front which was located on a mesa, and told to dig in. I recall the impossibility of "digging in." The ground was frozen solid. With my hands and my scoop, I did as best I could and had dug a little indentation when trouble began. My "Armageddon" had commenced.

It is difficult to describe the devastation and destruction caused by large artillery barrages directed at us. It was inconceivable anybody could survive this situation. With tremendous artillery resources the Germans turned their 88's at blank range on us. Constant shelling resulted in an absolute fire of death. The explosions were deafening. They spared no amount of shells. Every second the ground was literally exploding from under us. It was futile to place troops armed with rifles to a situation such as this. We did not see German foot soldiers at this time. It wasn't necessary for them to attack. It seemed every inch of the ground was being destroyed around and under us. There was considerable value in moving our group up as the Germans could not know our strength. In fact, they were diverted from moving forward, and apparently held back because of a decision from their higher-ups. I am sure they must have decided our little group had to be eliminated before they moved on. Eliminated we were. The concussion from the shells was so great that my hearing was permanently damaged. The barrages were so intense that it soon became obvious there was no possibility of our little rifles creating any diversion. However, we bought valuable time for our retreating groups.

One Jewish boy after about the fourth terrible barrage stood up and threw his hands to the heavens screaming in Hebrew, prayers for survival. You could see him in the dark night only as a silhouette as explosion light flashed. After the next barrage there were no more prayers, no more screams.

I was praying with intensity, as never before. I remember saying an Act of Contrition and other prayers and asking for deliverance. I remember asking that I might live because I wanted so badly to have a family of my own and live a normal life doing whatever I could. I particularly thought of my father. I was the only child. He had no one really close in the world except me.

The artillery barrages became more severe and intense. After a period of time, I became very angry -- angry at the stupidity of all this and of men destroying each other. Even angrier at a God who would not respond to His people (namely "me") crying out in anguish. I never had understood this kind of terrible suffering or the reason for it. My anger was very real and very positive. I had certainly led a good life (at least by my standards). During my teen years I had remained very close to the Roman Catholic Mass and the Sacraments. I couldn't understand why my God could allow this to happen to me.

Suddenly, reality set in. I was ashamed. We were

surrounded, outnumbered it appeared by more than ten to one. They had tremendous artillery power. We had little or none. There was absolutely no way out. Death was inevitable and there I was telling God how to run His universe. In my shame, I made a statement to God that I was ready to die with whatever pain or whatever He had in mind for me. "I fully accept Your will, I fully accept death with belief in You and in the eternal reward You have promised." The decision was made openly and completely. It was a voluntary giving of myself to the will of God. The graces immediately showered upon me were tremendous. This resignation to God's will was not made out of fear -- but strength. It was given happily and joyously. I then waited for the inevitable, strangely calm and filled with the Holy Spirit.

At that moment and almost immediately with that statement of resignation I was firmly swept up from the battlefield (as St. John states "whether in or out of the body I do not know,") into a state of ecstasy. The pain, the cold, the misery and the fear disappeared. They were replaced by, for want of better words, by the ultimate of security blankets. Never had I had a feeling like this before. Absolute and complete security and warmth. I was overwhelmed with love and joy, with feelings of being wanted and cared for. Simultaneously I was as if in a tunnel and was being propelled through the universe, the feeling of going hundreds of miles per hour and shooting through space was very strong but largely secondary because of the immensity of the power of love and happiness and ultimate joy. Also involved were some clacking sounds which I cannot explain. I felt myself leaving my body gently but firmly being pulled away.

Until I read the writings of Elizabeth Kubler-Ross many, many years later I forgot all about these small side effects. I do not know how long I was in this state of ecstasy, but I do recall the reverse of the shooting away from earth and kind of moving back toward earth at a fast pace. I also recall in the background, the sound of an artillery shell winging its way down upon me as I returned to the earth. It would appear that we both arrived simultaneously. I do not know how far the shell landed from me. It could not have been more than several feet. It was a dud. There was no explosion but my body was picked up and smashed to the earth and it seemed that I came back into my body and was fully cognizant at that very second as to what was happening, but without fear, apprehension or concern.

Anyone in the Infantry can tell you after thirty seconds of battle, if a shell has your number. You can tell from the sound and almost pick up the velocity and where the explosion is going to occur. This one was directly upon me. As I indicated it did not explode, although the velocity and reverberation threw me head first into the cold ground. I felt around the edge of the little hole of earth I had dug out and it seemed as if the earth was on fire around me.

It does little good for one who has experienced such events to use such words as joy, happiness, caring, love, concern, etc. because there is just absolutely no possible way one can convey the spirit and ecstasy of the moment. It was there and it was real. I have not told anyone of this experience and for over forty years have kept it completely within myself. Why I should now suddenly feel an urge to make this public in any way is beyond me. What happened, happened and the true story is herein told without amplification or embellishment.

No one can possibly make me believe that the forces of nature were not deliberately altered and changed by Almighty God. There is little doubt in my mind that that day could have been the date of my death. It could have then occurred had not supernatural forces intervened. It is hard for one to comprehend under the circumstances how anyone could have survived that battering.

I have no idea what all this meant. I certainly feel that it was not done because of me. I believe there must have been intervention of persons, living and/or dead, praying on my behalf. Whatever the cause I have no reason to believe I was as worthy or any worthier than comrades who met their demise that day. I have felt very strongly since that time that there had to be a special reason why I was spared. I have since lived a life on borrowed time, and that realization has never been out of my thoughts. I keep looking for some special mission or direction to evidence itself. While I have had a full and active life, certainly not devoid of some success, I have wondered what my mission is or was or whether the reason for being spared has yet to come about.

What has been recalled is only the beginning of an unbelievable story but the supernatural overtones of this one event have dramatically altered my life and for what it's worth is the keystone of what was to follow.

Let me bring up a couple of other points with regard to the miraculous events just described. I want to make it clear that prior to resignation as explained above, I was quite frightened and apprehensive. However, at no time was I out of control or in any way fantasizing. As I was lifted from the foxhole by a force so powerful yet so gentle, I had no fear, and no apprehension, just immediate feelings of love and fulfillment as above mentioned. I remember saying to myself "what in the hell is going on here?" Whenever a supernatural event is related there are always those who scoff or say that this was a product of the participants' imagination. I recall when I came back into my body and was thrown with great force to the ground simultaneously with the shell, I reached out from the foxhole, and said to myself "Lord, I will never again ever doubt your existence or your love."

At that point I do believe I was in complete union and filled with the Holy Spirit. From then on, I was a different person and any subsequent courageous activity was out of my individual control.

I have absolutely no idea how much time elapsed in that period. It could have been anywhere from minutes to hours. I have no way of knowing. It has to be remembered I was quite young. Events were occurring so rapidly that I did not have time to ask questions or fill in the usual details of all that was going on.

After I had been left alone at the roadblock our officers found out a large number of Nazi special troops had parachuted behind us, all dressed in American MP uniforms and all speaking impeccable English. These highly trained Nazis directed trucks and traffic the wrong way, turned directional signs around and created complete havoc in the mud and snow which stalled all traffic and made retreat very difficult. I'm sure that's why I was left with my Browning Automatic Rifle alone at that checkpoint and told to shoot if anybody came through, (American Uniform or not), without the proper password.

The above somewhat explains the chaos and loss of control as Hitler's "finest" pincered around our troops.

Getting back to the events at hand, shortly after the landing of the shell, there was a complete cessation of firing of guns and cannons. There was absolutely no sound around me.

It was but a few minutes when I heard someone calling my name. It was a friend of mine named Sylvan Greenhalgh, who could have been a part of the contingent who had volunteered to hold back the enemy. I responded to his call and he yelled, "Come on, Von, let's get the hell out of here."

I remember saying "what about the others?" His reply was "don't worry about them, they are all gone." I crawled from the foxhole and down the backside of a hill to a little valley where he was standing. There was a jeep there with the motor running; a colonel's expensive field coat was laying in it.

We walked and looked around. There was not a soul moving nor any sounds. I did not go back up the hill to look into the foxholes. We debated taking the jeep and/or leaving it as it was. All others had either fled or had been killed. We found no living beings.

The two of us then took off on foot, and slipped down some back roads in the direction we thought was away from the enemy. My friend took the officer's coat and put it on. We were freezing to death. The little jackets held no warmth.

We walked quite a way down the road and came to a fork which we didn't recognize. He wanted to go one way and I said we should go the other way. When we had arrived that night in trucks with lights turned out, turning right, left, and about, there was no way to keep any active track as to how we got there. I made the decision to go in the direction to the right and he went in the direction to the left. We agreed we would go our separate ways and if either found he was going in the wrong direction he would attempt to get back.

I walked alone through the hills and vales of Alsace Lorraine. It was for a considerable period of time. As I reached the top of a hill there came into view a beautiful multi story stone farm house. It was located on a high knoll.

By that time I was extremely exhausted. I had been up for 24 hours and desperately needed to get at least a few minutes of sleep. I approached the house. The door opened and the family in residence all crowded around. I couldn't talk the language and they couldn't speak English. By motions I indicated that I was weary and needed to have a few minutes rest and they nodded and took me into the house. The house was immaculately clean. Several generations of this family were present, six to eight people in all; all of whom were dressed and up even though the light of day had just barely broken through the dark night. The grandfather waved his hand and said something to a young teenager who took me upstairs to a beautiful bedroom. In the room was a double bed with goose down pillows and blankets. The house was just immaculate and the room was beautiful. I remember sitting down and taking my shoes off and collapsing on the bed. I had my gun by my side and fell asleep immediately. The next thing I recall, the young girl was shaking me frantically. I woke up immediately and looked up at her. With a frightened face she said the hated word "Bosch", their name for the German soldiers.

As I indicated before, the house was high on a knoll and I was on the second story. I immediately ran to the window and looked out. There was a magnificent panoramic view of the entire area in front of me which extended for what seemed to be several miles. As far as I could see in any direction were advancing German infantrymen in great depth with five or six tanks in the immediate area, and artillery in back of them. This was a most unbelievable sight. Even to this day I can only think of the old Indian movies when the cowboys would look up and see from high on the hill all the Indians by the thousands in every direction.

Obviously, there were thousands of troops coming up from the East marching in the direction of and toward the farmhouse and only a few hundred yards away. The only American combatant on the other side was me. With odds of many thousand to one it was a little ridiculous to stand and look out the window.

I frantically got into my shoes, grabbed my equipment and raced down the stairs.

The poor family was huddled together arms around each other. There was terror in the eyes of each of them. They full well knew the fate that was before them, especially for the women and girls. I moved quickly to the front door. I noticed a number of religious pictures, crucifixes on the wall. Not being able to talk to them, I quickly said thank you and for some reason gave them a sign of the cross blessing as I walked out the door. I will never know what happened to them.

At least I now knew the direction I should go and that was opposite the forces who were approaching. I went through the barn yard, down through the draws, the creeks and rivers, through the woods and cut across clearings using the protection of the house and the contours of the land to keep from being seen by the fast approaching troops. The advance German scouts would only be a few yards from the house by now.

As I cleared through to an open area, I found a pathway and trotted quickly down and over some hills. During all of this time, I had an unbelievable calm. However, the adrenalin was running. Every instinct was working and moving through my body and brain. I was as alert as I have ever been in my life thinking and weighing possibilities calmly in spite of the situation. As I came over a hill, some ten or fifteen minutes later, I saw three soldiers stand up and begin waving their hands. They were dug in immediately in front of me. Now for the next unbelievable miracle. They were not only American troops, but my company, platoon and squad. In spite of all of the areas and directions my aimless wanderings had taken me, I had walked into this small group of people whom I knew. The odds against this happening were beyond belief. It was a pleasant reunion and my squad welcomed me. Everyone had thought I was dead by now. We quickly reviewed all the things that had happened since we had last been together.

Immediately our Captain and another officer, I think a Colonel from Intelligence or from the Division came up and began interrogating me as to what I had seen out there. I calmly explained the situation and the thousands of Nazi troops shortly in back of me. They began asking precise questions as to how many, where, how far and brought out maps for me to show exactly where I thought they might be. I directed them, being careful to direct fire past and away from the farm house. Within seconds by virtue of telephone conversation back, our huge artillery shells were whistling over our heads and going out to slow down the enemy. I knew and explained that I had only seen a small part of them and that this was one gigantic movement and attack against us.

I then learned we were completely surrounded by German troops; including elite SS troops. There was no known avenue of escape. Our troops had just come up and began to dig in. I rejoined my squad and did likewise.

The artillery blasts surprised the German troops and temporarily stopped them. My information was most accurate and they altered their plan of attack. They began counter barrages but attack was delayed until the next morning. We would have been annihilated if they had pursued their attack at that time.

Fortunately, in the meantime, we had been directed to move to our left which probably would have been to the North before they came in. Those few that didn't get out were immediately shot and killed by their tanks. We moved in the Northerly direction and stayed that night lying on the ground. We were about frozen to death and there was no food. The next morning we continued on to the top of a large hill. Our artillery had bogged down the approaching Nazis coming from the East. We had bought valuable time. The artillery fire which I had directed apparently messed up their plans or at least their timing.

We came to the top of another hill. Immediately artillery and rifle shooting began. We were ordered to dig in to the ground again. I remembered digging a fox hole and sharing same with an American Indian boy. His name was Allen. Anyway, we dug a double fox hole as fast as we could. The Nazis were now dumping mortar fire on us together with the fire from the 88's. Again the tremendous bombarding of our position began. It was so bad that I could hear nothing when it was through. My ears were reverberating or echoing the blasts and the high pitch noises were quite powerful and painful. Our officers were urging us to attack and proceed up the hill as fast as we could go. Most of us temporarily stayed in our fox holes because the ongoing tremendous bombardment made it impossible to move. The bullets and shrapnel were whistling by my head. Through it all with everybody covering up as best they could, there came a lone man zig-zagging his way up the hill running, then hitting the ground, and getting up to run again in a crouched position.

As was my want, I reacted quickly, I yelled at him "you silly S.O.B., get over here in the foxhole." He ran over and jumped in the fox hole with us. Obviously he knew that the odds were against his getting much further. I remember berating him for the stupidity of not staying down when all of this was going on. At that point he said, "I happen to be your battalion commander."

I shut up. PFC's did not reserve such names for Colonels and remain happy warriors. It wasn't the first time my big mouth had gotten me in trouble (and it sure wasn't the last) I felt stupid. About 40 seconds later, notwithstanding the exploding shells, he leaped out of the fox hole and began zig-zagging up the hill to our right.

The bombardment continued on. Our Company officers were urging us to come out. We were going to do the only decent thing we could do and that was to attack. When you are surrounded and being destroyed, there wasn't an alternative. I moved cautiously out of the fox hole and crawled up to the top of the hill along with a number of my other friends. Most all of my good buddies were within yards of me at that time. All of a sudden an officer said "let's go" and we started up again. We were at the crest of the hill and running forward. I saw two of my friends go down within ten feet of me. There were dead people lying all over the place. I hit the ground again and stayed as low as I could. Where were these people shooting from? I could not ascertain where they were but they were fantastic marksmen. Two of my friends had been shot between the eyes and were dead before they hit the ground. I knew this as I observed the way they fell and did not move. With increasing anger, I cautiously looked up and about trying to ascertain where the fire was coming from. There was a big farmhouse right in front of us, a grove of trees and some bushy area. We could not see where the barrages were coming from, however. I finally decided that enough was enough. We were being picked off one by one. If I were going to die it wasn't by lying with my head in the snow. I got up and slung the strap of the BAR over my shoulder. (This was a big and heavy rifle. You were supposed to shoot it from a prone position). I just laid it against my hip and started running into the enemy. With my finger on the trigger, I sprayed shots against the farm house, the barn, the trees; any direction where they might be holed up. My move directed their fire power toward me. I could feel and hear the bullets flying by my head and steeled myself for the inevitable impact against my body. It never came.

I fell heavily a couple of times because of the slick snow and the sharp incline but I kept moving forward, crawling and standing up and shooting. I was now really drawing the fire of the enemy and again could feel the bullets and shrapnel whizzing by. My rapid automatic rifle was spitting bullets until empty. As I reached for another ammunition magazine and slammed it into the BAR, I heard the Captain shouting to cease fire. Unbelievably they had gone. They had retreated. I stood there in kind of a daze and let my gun slip to the ground. Redundant details of the battle are omitted.

I was surrounded by bodies of fallen comrades,

intermixed with German soldiers. People were running up to me and screaming at me and patting me on the back. I can remember one guy, a fellow from Philadelphia, named Kelly, a very brave soldier who later received a battlefield commission, running over and grabbing me saying "you saved my life, they had me." I was an instant hero.

It was sheer anger and frustration that had forced me forward. We had been trained never to do anything like I had done. In any event, I was alive; all of my friends were dead.

By this time I was calm and relaxed, without fear or concern and I then did a very strange thing. I walked over to a place where a young German soldier was laying dead. I had checked out the bodies of my friends. The medics were now coming up and removing bodies. I took my helmet off, sat down on it and pulled out a C-ration. I think it was cold ham and eggs. I sat there eating, staring at this guy. I can't really explain why I did that. It all added to the legend because I had literally walked through the "valley of death" and not been scratched. (Everybody had assumed that I had been killed earlier. but I had walked around and past and through several thousand Germans). Now I was in a category of a strange but very lucky soldier who was brave and cool. Apparently this message was sent out as I ate my C-rations and sat on the helmet. Everything had happened so fast.

I went back to the fox hole. There was my friend Allen sitting in the fox hole just as I had left him. I went over and jumped in, said "what in the hell are you doing here, why didn't you come out?" His body slumped against me. He was dead. If I had stayed there, I undoubtedly would have also been killed.

At that point the lieutenant came running up to me and said "I'm writing you up for a medal for this." About a minute later our Captain (who was wounded later that day) came over and excitedly said "I'm recommending you for a medal." I have to admit I was overwhelmed with the whole situation, but wasn't concerned about medals. We were trapped. Shortly thereafter the Captain came back and said we just have been radioed that the Nazis are moving back into the South and some trucks have gotten through to get us out of here. That is exactly what happened. Those of us who survived were immediately moved from the area, but all of my immediate and close friends were dead.

Even as I dictate this, it is hard for me to believe all of this happened.

When I was sitting there on my helmet eating my cold scrambled eggs, a couple of the guys came up and said: "Aren't you a little cold?"

I replied "Of course I'm cold, aren't you?" They said "yes, but have you seen the back of your jacket?"

I took my jacket off and looked at it. There was no back in it. It was in shreds from shrapnel. My solid steel helmet had a dent in it the size of a small orange which almost seems impossible. You could pound a helmet with hammers and not do that. The left pocket of my pants was shot open and my leg was bare. In that pocket were my glasses. The case of the glasses was ripped by a bullet which hit the case and ricocheted off. I had been hit by another ricochet bullet, but I can't remember precisely where. I think it bounced off something hard that I had in my pocket up around my chest area. It was not uncommon for infantry men to have some bullet marks in clothing. I had just about been undressed. I didn't have a scratch.

Later on when I had time, the fright came back and I trembled a bit as I recalled the events of the day.

Once again, I had to pause to give thanks to the Lord and to ask the question how and why was I still alive. This was absolutely impossible.

The dead German soldier I had been staring at was very young, an officer and, I believe, an SS man. He had classic Teutonic features with a strong well chiseled face and blonde hair. I could only look at him and think that obviously there were parents or sweethearts who would grieve. He probably didn't hate anybody anymore than I did.

The seeds of discontent were beginning to build. If you are an infantry man exposing your life for others, it doesn't take much in the way of brains to figure out that this is a hapless task; that you are totally expendable; and in the final analysis, you are the dummy who is being sacrificed or given up for the cause.

War is so stupid. Why and how can human beings do this to each other.

At that particular time we didn't have any idea as to the tremendous impact of this battle. We knew the

German attack was big and we knew it was an important factor in the war, but the size and scope of the whole thing was a bit beyond our comprehension. We were too close to the actual struggle.

We moved back quickly and regrouped as best we could. My timing of events may be a little off but we were well aware that 422nd regiment and 423rd regiment or two thirds of our division was gone -- either dead, wounded or captured. The 424th regiment was all alone.

At that point the 106th division was disbanded and we continued in battle as the 424th Regimental Combat Team.

We were to be at the disposal of the key generals of the allied command to fill in wherever there was an emergency or wherever we were needed. As a result, our regiment ended up fighting battles under the directorship of Field Marshal Montgomery of England, General Omar Bradley, General Hodge of the First Army, and General George Patton of the Third Army.

We were passed around continually without relief from front line action and except for a couple of days were at the front from December 16, 1944 through April 15, 1945, the day I subsequently left the Company.

There wasn't time to think of attire but I indeed must have been a pretty sight. I described the condition of my clothes. In addition, I was still carrying the BAR, had bandoleers of bullets cross draped across my neck, three hand grenades attached to my jacket, a regular ammunition belt with my knife pouch empty, the knife had been left back at the intersection that I was guarding. I was a walking powder keg. Thank God I didn't get hit or I could have blown up on the spot.

To finish off the surprises of my first 72 hours of warfare, I was called in by a new Captain shortly after backing off from the front line.

"Vonachen," he said, "we put your name in for sergeant." "But Sir, I don't want--" "Never mind, I am not asking you, I'm telling you. This is the position we want you in."

I was taken aback. I had become rather comfortable in doing my own thing and using my brain and athletic ability to save myself from harm. The thought of being responsible for a dozen or so other people blew my mind.

It wasn't that I didn't think I could do it or that I didn't have confidence in my leadership ability. In fact in my brash young mind it never occurred to me that I couldn't handle the job. However, the thought of my making decisions which could mean the life or death of many people had just never occurred to me. I had harbored no thoughts of ever being a non-commissioned officer. Since I had just turned nineteen and was one of the youngest men in the Company, it did present somewhat of a problem because I would be dealing with men whose ages for the most part ran from twenty-one through twenty-eight years. Yet, a Sergeant was an Assistant Squad Leader and did not have full responsibility of running the Squad.

I nodded my assent. Then came the crowning blow. "You are taking over the 4th Squad. We don't have Staff Sergeants now and you will be the Squad Leader until we tell you differently."

This ended my cop-out position. He walked away before I had a chance to say anything further, except to note that my Squad was pretty battered. He replied: "We have reserves coming up and will fill out your spots immediately. I'll let you know when the orders are approved." We then moved back and regrouped our fast dwindling forces.

We stayed in the basement of a farm house which had one side blown out. The chimney was still operating and there was a fire in the fireplace. The Squad slept around the open basement which at least gave us more protection than we had had since the beginning of fighting. Farm animals were lying dead in the area. Seeing cows with their feet sticking straight up the air with rigor mortis having set in is enough to turn your stomach for some time. The place was a mess. Obviously there had been a great deal of artillery fire here. We still had nothing to eat. There were no supplies coming up.

Some soldiers cut a loin out of a dead cow and cooked it. Those who ate became violently ill. We were in the throes of starvation, diarrhea and vomiting. I had turned down meat from the cow and did not get ill.

We reorganized as best we could and soon were sent back to another sector of the front. My squad was spread among hedge rows. In order to get to them from the Company command post, I had to crawl and take cover. I had been called from the front and was back a couple of blocks when the Captain came up and informed me that I had been approved as Sergeant. He gave me insignia which was a wide tape mark which adhered to the back of my helmet. We, and I'm sure the Germans also, had been taught that when in combat you try to kill the squad leader as soon as possible; therefore this tape mark on the back of the helmet was the only indication of rank.

As we were talking, there was a shot from the front and screams. It was from my squad. I ran from the Captain, hit the ground and crawled to the front.

A lad who had gone through basic training with was in his foxhole screaming. I crawled up to him and jumped in.

He screamed, "Bud, I didn't mean to do it, I didn't mean to do it."

I looked down. He had blown half of his foot off by accident.

Shooting yourself was a cardinal sin for an infantry man. We had always been informed if a person in combat shot himself, especially in the toe or any extremity, unless it could be proven to the contrary, it was assumed to have been deliberate.

I immediately got him out of the foxhole. The medics came up and carted him away. He was a good and brave soldier. I had no doubt in my mind that it was an accident, and have often wondered what happened to him and how he was treated under the circumstances.

It is important at this point to also mention that in the course of events there were many soldiers who threw down rifles and ran. There were several who deliberately shot themselves counting on going through life with an injury rather than risking death. One shooting in particular I knew was not an accident because the soldier involved had confided to me before battle that he intended this if it got too rough. I hadn't believed him until I heard of his intentional injury.

Perhaps those facts can convey just a bit of the horror and fright that can overtake a person.

As I looked back upon the earlier events, it was very hard for me to believe that I had deliberately exposed myself to enemy fire and, of course, probable death during the last battle. By standing up I had deliberately directed all of the fire power toward myself. I don't know how other people felt about it but I certainly didn't do it for God, Country, medals or any of that. I guess motivation was for my friends' well-being and involved a very intense feeling of brotherly love, duty and responsibility. Even though I had known these individuals only a couple of months, there had built up a tremendous caring and respect for them. I realize that isn't a very satisfactory answer and maybe others had different feelings about that sort of activity. To me, the bond between infantry men is one that is simply beyond explanation. Where lives are concerned you quickly move toward the common good, whatever the cost and almost without thinking you find that indeed you are your brother's keeper.

I also must point out that continuously since the

out of body experience I had acted fearlessly and spontaneously when crisis was involved. The Holy Spirit of God guided me through the tough times. Fear and apprehension only hit me after the imminent danger had passed.

A factor which made it easier for me was the fact that I had been with an anti-tank company for most of my pre-combat training. Only a month before going overseas I was transferred to B Company of the 424th Infantry. As a result, I did not have usual close association and longevity of friendship with my peers at the time of the Bulge. This made it much easier for me to accept the deaths and injuries of those who had fallen. I quickly had come to the conclusion that one is better off not to have too many close friendships especially if in a leadership position.

The Captain then asked me if I would lead a patrol into an enemy town. It was a little village between the rolling hills of Alsace Lorraine. He indicated that intelligence was 98% sure the town was evacuated but he wanted somebody to take four or five soldiers down, sneak into the town and made sure there were no Germans left. I indicated that I would do it.

A bit later an intelligence officer from another division came up with the Captain. We got into a jeep and they took me to the top of a high hill where, with binoculars, we could look down on this town. It was a quaint village nestled in the hills. The only way to get to it from any direction was to go down these vales without cover to check the buildings nestled in the valley below. It was very small with only a few dozen houses. I stayed there a long time hiding behind rocks and looking down on the town. Something was wrong. I could instinctively tell there was trouble but I couldn't put my finger on the problem. It was obvious the town had not yet been a battle site. Nevertheless, no one was going back and forth between any houses. There was not a soul to be seen. If it were not occupied, there surely would have been somebody out of the houses once in a while. At any rate, we observed the town for several days and planned on maps the routes that we were to take. We were to leave about 1:00 a.m. in the morning under the cover of night, sneak into town and check it out. It was not our purpose to confront the enemy but simply to gain information as to what was going on. I prepared my people. At the last second the trip was scrubbed. The intelligence group had been wrong again and there were 220 Germans in the town with surrounding machine gun nests in the areas where we were to go. This was the third time in a couple of days Corps intelligence had failed. I was disgusted toward that group and was too young to keep my mouth shut. Events in the future would show that they were not a help but a hindrance to our very lives.

Back again at the front, all of us were in position waiting for additional enemy attack when a truck came careening down the road. It was my friend Mike Ryan. We had been roommates at the University of Wisconsin. The truck approached our position with screeching brakes came to a halt. "Where's Vonachen."

I answered and we had a quick talk about the events of the days just gone by. Mike was a cook for one of the companies and had pretty much taken the truck on his own and gone back to get some food for his people who were starving just as we were. He found out the supply people of the U.S. Army back in Paris were taking the food that was to go to us. With the bedlam that came from the Bulge they were selling our food on the black market in Paris. Needless to say this was disconcerting. I asked if he had any food and Mike replied that all he had was a few cans of grapefruit juice. They turned out to be 32 oz. cans. He gave those cans to us. We had had no food for a long time so we drank the juice. It was a great and welcome repast. Mike again took off. That was the last I saw him until after the war. After we finished the grapefruit juice we all ended up with dysentery. Now we were not only starving but could hardly stand up.

Christmas Day 1944 was a special day. I remember in the early morning on my stomach in some farmland close to Aachen. Of course, the fact that this area is the family name source made it special. At that time I was terribly hungry and very cold. I was sopping wet from top to bottom and the chill was from a wind that seemed to literally go right through you. As I lay in that farmland I dug with my hands down to what I suppose was the roots from Brussels sprouts, pulling them up, cleaning them in the snow and eating the sprouts.

Here we were cold, lonely and without hope of removing ourselves from the web. We were again trapped. Yet I never felt closer to God, nor could I remember a Christmas when the coming of Christ meant more to me; I can still say that to this day. Again, I prayed that God's will be done but also that there be some special way I could show my love for the Lord in the days to come. No restrictions or favors were asked this time.

The 7th Armored Division had moved up. We climbed on the back of their tanks and attacked the Germans. They were so numerically superior that we could not prevail. I can only assume that our move confused them. This type of activity by Americans had a great deal to do with turning the tide of the Battle of the Bulge. We would hit and run. Our division was constantly doing things that made no sense and every time we did the unpredictable, the Germans sat back and puzzled over what to do next rather than just moving ahead and cleaning us out. They could have done that very simply.

Even the cooks and the utility men grabbed rifles and were moving up into the line. Although we were fighting big guns and tanks with what would appear to be popguns, we caused delay and held the Germans to the point that their timetable was completely upset; our needed replacements were given time to get in place and shore up the defenses.

Additional daily battles and patrols were eventful but nothing terribly exciting. We settled down to a routine holding position.

I took my new responsibilities very seriously and was very critical and demanding. It is impossible not to make enemies when you are constantly questioning the wisdom of superiors. To be honest, I felt I was smarter than many of those who were giving me orders and had a great deal more common sense than those calling the shots. This made for difficult relationships and some hard feeling. Unfortunately at that time the virtue of humility had escaped me.

Nonetheless I became very cynical as I realized that the infantry men were just cannon fodder for ambitious generals, and that my frequent patrols were sent only to draw fire to satisfy "Intelligence." The value of a human life to some in command was nil.

The only time that I can recall not immediately and effectively reacting to somebody in trouble was in the course of an attack along the edge of one of the great forests in the Ardennes. We had been instructed to stay under the cover of the forest even though walking was treacherous and difficult because of underbrush. One of the soldiers moved out of the forest and into an adjoining field simply to avoid the difficulty in moving.

A machine gun opened fire and he was hit. He dropped in the middle of the open field. My Squad and I were directly opposite him about a quarter of a block away up in the forest area. His screams for help were indeed heart rendering and I gathered my squad and said: "I have to help that boy. You guys stay right here."

At that point his cries for help were beginning to become fainter and fainter. He subsequently started to regress and was calling for his mother.

Telling each member of the squad to wait there that I would be right back I started out for the open field. To get to him was almost suicidal but I felt a deep obligation to try. At that point a large hand grabbed me from the back of my shoulder and I heard: "Sergeant, you're not going anywhere -- your responsibility is this squad and you do not leave them." It was one of the Company Officers who had overheard my comments.

He was right, of course, in that by not being a team player, I could be acting in a manner detrimental to the welfare of the people under my command.

He commanded all of us to go to the edge of the woods and start a barrage of fire along the woods as much and as fast as we could in order to make the machine gunners take cover. We did just that.

About twenty minutes later, the word came down that the boy's body had been recovered. He had been shot through the heart and actually drowned in his own blood as it moved into his lungs. Although, from another company, he was a soldier that I had run around with and a friend of mine. I did not know who it was at the time. To this day the haunting refrain of his cries, calls for help, screams of anguish, and at the end in tears, calling to his mother for help, live with me. Those echoes will live with me all of my days.

By the middle of January the Germans were pushed back and the intense fighting was over.

My squad re-enforcements came. Mostly they were Tennessee hillbillies. They could shoot the eye of a squirrel at 200 yards, but really were the most messed up and disorganized army people I had ever seen. My days with them were a study of cursing, cajoling, pleading and violence. This group of characters could not have fit in at the country club socials.

They never did learn about the safety catch on rifles, how to handle themselves personally to survive the winter, or common sense tactics like not crossing in front of somebody shooting in combat. There is no question after a couple of weeks I was completely frustrated.

Some of them could not say a sentence without a four letter word and believe me, they knew them all. This was my squad. Surprisingly, I became quite fond of many of them.

In all candor, I must say that I was not exactly the astute soldier and role model. While my instincts and directions were well founded, I was not what you could call a classic leader. Our relationship ended at times in confrontations and battles, alienating certain of the squad. I was very tough on them and demanded strict adherence to my rules. It does little good to go into details at this point other than to say I spent hours with them trying to make them into soldiers. I was a dismal flop. In all fairness many of them should not have been in the front lines. As subsequent replacements came up, I found them far more inept soldiers than my Tennessee boys.

During the days that followed, we were constantly at the beck and call of the Generals above named. In one battle situation after another, we were plugged in where needed. Most of our fights were around the Maginot line. The cold was just fierce. I can recall nights when it was so cold, well below zero, that we would burn ourselves to get close to fires in order to keep life going. One night in particular I ran and climbed trees just to be moving and avoid the temptation to lay down and fall into a sleep from which one might not awaken.

I kept an extra pair of socks in my shorts at all times. My body heat would dry them out. I would change socks two or three times a day.

I would require my men to take off their shoes and let me look at their feet. Usually, I would ask if their feet were cold and hurting. If they said no, I made them take their shoes off. I sent some men back whose feet had turned completely black. I was told that the hospitals would immediately cut their feet off because if this was not quickly done, gangrene would set in. We truly suffered. God, how we suffered.

Yet we turned the situation around. We were beginning to drive back the Germans. Our motley group would attack when we should have fallen back; ignore all odds, do battle when it made no sense and confuse the enemy by hit and run tactics. We stopped the Nazi juggernaut. We confused them.

One day we were sent on attack against the Germans. Patton was our Field Commander and we were told to go very lightly as far as dress was concerned because there was no stopping or turning back. We took off and had several skirmishes. After a bit, the Germans zeroed in on us with big cannons. We were spread out in battle attack and pressed forward. There were sporadic bombardments from 88's, whose shells were timed to explode in the air and in the trees sending forth not only their deadly shrapnel but also hunks of wood through the air. This was a most extreme battle and really tough going.

There was a quiet in the shooting. At that point several soldiers brought a young man to me. They were not from my squad. They said "Sergeant, we have to do something with Bob here; he is really sick." I took one look at him and I knew this was so.

He was a young man from Texas, a very fine soldier. We had played football against each other in England. He was indeed a tough guy.

I said, "Bob, come here," and I put my hand to his head. His eyes were glazed. He was carrying a very high fever.

I said "open your jacket." He did so and I felt his chest which was burning up also. Obviously, he had an acute upper respiratory situation and possible pneumonia. I noticed that all he had on covering his upper body was a shirt and a little field jacket. Unless protected with more than that, one just could not survive in these environs.

I directed the soldiers to immediately bring up a medic so we could evacuate him.

The medic came up and said: "Sorry Sergeant, General Patton has issued orders that nobody is to be relieved of duty unless they are carried out."

Bob was not my responsibility and yet in a way he was. I can't recall why he didn't have a sergeant of his own to take charge of him but in any event, there was nobody else available.

Recalling my Christmas day pledge to Our Lord, I

knew immediately what I had to do. "Please, Lord, please don't ask this of me." I prayed. There was no answer.

I took him aside and went back into the woods with him as I didn't want anybody else to see. I again asked: "Please Lord, relieve me of this responsibility." Again I knew what I had to do.

I was thinking back to that Christmas Eve night when I asked for something special that I might do.

Finally, I told Bob to take his coat off. I took mine off and gave him my sweater.

I can only say that sweater was more important to me at that time than a million dollars. It was a token of life retention. It represented the possible warmth and protection to fight your way through this dreadful pain and cold. I did not want to give it to him.

Yet I couldn't go back on my gift offer. I had no opportunity to squirm out of it and still live with myself.

Bob looked at me with disbelief. I said "put it on" and "can you hold on and make it?" He nodded. I sent him back to his squad.

About that time orders came to move on. It was only a matter of fifteen or twenty minutes later when another barrage came. About 40 feet from me I heard terrible screams. I ran over. It was Bob. A hunk of wood bigger than my hand had been shrapnelized by the explosion of an 88 shell. It was sticking in his leg which was bared to the bone. He was screaming in agony.

We did the best we could to clean out the wound and put sulfa powder in to keep infection down.

I can remember them taking him away. It was the same medic. At least we found a way to get Bob back. As he was lifted up and taken away, to my everlasting dishonor, all I saw was my sweater departing.

At this point one tends to over dramatize the situation. I had underwear and adequate other clothes that gave me enough to get by on. But that precious sweater was very important in my mind.

We started again on attack and I walked through the chilling wind and continuing cold. I have never felt better about myself before or since. The joy and love of Christ lifted me with a holy exhilaration. I walked into the unknown and possible death. But on that one day, at least, I knew in my heart that Our Lord was well pleased with me.

I don't want to magnify this into something more than it is, yet I can't recall from that day forward really suffering from the cold again as we moved our way through various battles in Northern France. This is the first time I have ever told this entire story. I might add that for over 45 years this has been my secret with the Lord. It was done privately because to use it might unjustly magnify my worth in some people's eyes. I tell it now only because of the tremendous joy and happiness it gave me to give up something I wanted so badly for the sake of Jesus Christ. It was a lesson I learned and want to pass on to my children and grandchildren.

I was beginning to lose it though and I knew it. My shoulder hurt very badly from my earlier days with the automatic rifle, my knee kept locking and my hearing was beginning to fail. There was a terrible ringing in my ears at all times from the explosion of shells. The continuing cold was taking its toll on the joints of all of us.

In the course of events, I had alienated additional people, including a couple of officers. I was pretty discouraged and absolutely devastated at the thought of this going on much longer.

It all seemed an eternity. There could not be any just war. I knew that now. To allow these sacrificial lambs, namely us, to continue to be set up to promote the folly of man just blew my mind. At that point I had no alternate approach to suggest and certainly nobody would have listened to me if I had. I was not close to any of these people, it was just a very difficult time, and the constant life and death tension was getting to me. We did know our cause was just and honorable; that the world would be in turmoil if we failed.

I spent more and more time with my men on guard duty at the perimeter of the Hürtgen forest. I would sleep for an hour and then join the guy out in the lookout foxhole. At that time I was smoking over three packs of cigarettes a day; I can't believe I was that stupid. But that's the way life was and is for the infantrymen. I shared with my squad the deepest of feelings. We talked of death, their families and our responsibilities. Again the bond which resulted is unexplainable. The duty relationship between combat soldiers and a sort of love is one that can't be explained to third parties. It was not a personal thing; it was just there and a duty to be met.

One Sergeant in particular (who outranked me) was very unfriendly. I had a couple of verbal clashes with him and really didn't know what his big problem was. He certainly disliked me. On the day in question we had taken over one of the concrete bunkers in the Maginot line and were staying there overnight.

On entering, I bumped into this fellow inadvertently. With a great outburst of profanity he questioned my ancestry. I looked up in disbelief. He was standing there and had a knife in his hand. I completely lost control, dove at him and drove him into the ground. Fortunately there were a number of people there to ultimately stop us. I had his head in my hands and was pounding it on the concrete floor. Three or four guys pulled me off of him. I was screaming out of control. I might have killed him if they hadn't stopped me.

I still recall threatening that if I ever caught him within twenty feet of me again in any direction he would be eating dinner for the rest of his life through a straw. Later I sat on my bunk and tried to figure out what was happening to me. This certainly was not me nor anything I would ever want to be. Just the opposite. I was losing control of myself and also wasn't a very good example for my men, to say the least. I tell this story more in shame than anything else because although he had egged me on, this is certainly not what I stood for or how I would want to be remembered. I will say this, as I looked into his eyes that night when it was over, I knew I would never be bothered with him again. I wasn't.

We now knew the extent of the Bulge, what had happened to us and that for all practical purposes it was over. I received a great deal of mail from home. My dad wrote me every day and an increasing number of friends wrote me. We were instructed to bury all mail when we got through with it because supposedly it would give the Germans information. I can recall getting clippings of the war and even personal clippings of what had happened to some of the Peoria boys, including myself. One clipping in particular was indeed painful. This involved a clipping by Drew Pearson who was one of the leading columnists of the time stating how the 106th Division "like straws in the wind" had dissolved in front of the Germans. I don't know where he got his information but the whole disgrace of the thing as I read the article was more than I or my friends (those few left) who had been there from the beginning, could handle. Knowing what had really happened, and the gallantry and personal destruction of so many friends, I just sat down and cried.

Every night about dusk they threw their heavy artillery at us. This happened for some weeks on end. Our side would respond. The opposing Germans were so close that we took some of our own shells. The bombardments were not very effective but mentally took their toll in all of us.

Shortly before we were relieved from the front we came across unbelievably heavy foggy weather in the Hürtgen Forest. One of the officers came down from the command post and asked to see me. He said they had lost complete contact with the American troops to the left of us. He asked me if I would volunteer to take out a patrol to see if we could make contact with the troops on the other side of us. The Hürtgen Forrest, and I can't emphasize this enough, was totally black at night. You literally couldn't see your hands in front of your face in places and it was an almost impossible task for anybody to leave his post and know where he was going. He also indicated there was German activity somewhere between the other group and ourselves. We would have to go through no man's land to make contact.

They had sent out three other patrols and each of the three had gotten lost and had to come back. I said I would do it provided that it be done the way I wanted. (By this time I was completely obnoxious). I required two of the very top infantry men with the company to aid and go with me; we would not take any equipment with us except small rifles and ammunition; the Lieutenant would personally see that all of the troops in the front lines were told and understood that we were going out and would be coming back sometime within the next hour or so. This was terribly important because by this time everyone had the jitters. Apparently the Germans had trained numbers of German Shepard dogs to harass enemy troops. There were German patrols sighted in the area also. We had to go out in front of and beyond the front lines in order to cut through to contact our own troops. Finally, it was determined by radio that a patrol from the neighboring division would be sent at the same time. We established something in the way of a signal to each other to let the other know from a distance that everything was alright so long as we could make contact.

With the two young men who were assigned I took off. Fortunately, I had studied the ground contours during the daylight hours and as best as I could tell had fairly well mastered the nearby hills and valleys. I have no idea how long we were out. We went to the front lines and then after alerting everybody went slowly down the hill into no-man's land. We weren't out but several minutes when we got lost and I found later that we had been walking in circles. The whole situation was kind of crazy because it was so dark. Neither side could have mounted any kind of a meaningful offensive or diversionary tactic. In any event, we plodded on. I was absolutely determined that I was going to make contact and was not coming back until we had communication with our troops to our left.

The tactic of the German Army always had been to use a pincer's movement in isolating the enemy and this was what the command feared. We moved slowly and deliberately. I kept track of every nook and cranny trying to give an image of reversal so that we could find our way back. It was impossible to see more than a couple of feet in front. About twenty minutes out I heard a noise and grabbed my two companions. We had agreed to keep within touch distance of each other under the circumstances. I held my finger to each of their mouths and we stood perfectly still. A squad of eight to eleven or more Germans then passed us. They were going uphill and were bent forward. They were so close several of them brushed by me. I recall looking back at my companions. They were paralyzed. The fright in their eyes was apparent. I have never seen two kids more scared in my life. The whole situation struck me as rather humorous and I soundlessly was shaking with laughter. It was time to get out when you found humor in a life/death situation such as this.

At any rate the Germans passed on and all I really heard from them was grunts and the clacking of their boots as they moved forward. As soon as they had passed, we immediately moved in the opposite direction, across creeks and other wooded areas and ultimately came within hearing distance of our counterpart patrol coming from the other direction. We gave the designated signals to each other across a body of water and then started back. I was satisfied that nothing negative would come from the enemy that might. Returning to our lines presented two problems. The first was whether we would contact the German patrol again and secondly, if not, would we be able to even find our way back. We started off and after a substantial period of time got back. We had completed our patrol, made our contact and I assured the officers at the command post that whatever the German squad was doing down there, they weren't going to bother anybody because they couldn't see anything anyway. Also, our troops on the other side of us were secure. We now knew there was no big enemy movement between us. In coming back I don't recall any big problem. The patrol had gone off without a great deal of difficulty.

The next morning a couple officers and myself went to the outpost from which my patrol had left and slid down the hill into the draw the night before. One of the officers was from Corps Intelligence. We got to the top of the hill and down below was the area where we had initially become lost and had walked in circles. Our footprints in the snow were all over the place.

The guy stopped and gasped, "My God, who in the hell was walking down there? We have completely mined that area." I don't think I need explain at this point my reaction to all of this, to the embarrassment and consternation of the officer of our Company. I couldn't believe this was happening to me. How many times did these people screw up a situation. Another miracle. I know it sounds crazy but that's the way it happened.

We had not only walked through a concentrated mine field, but gone in circles through it.

That evening I was called to the Command Post again for something and in coming back, it now being dark, I heard footsteps behind me. I walked a few more feet and threw myself to the ground behind a tree, cocking my rifle.

The guy immediately started screaming "Sergeant, it's me, Lou. I've been walking behind you since you left the Command Post." This was about a block to a block and a half walk. The realization came upon me at this point that I had for all practical purposes lost my hearing now. The high pitch noise in my ears was so bad that I couldn't tell when somebody who wasn't even trying to be quiet was walking through the forest behind me. It turned out among the other lasting physical problems I had permanently lost one third of my hearing.

These events added to the futility of the situation, my feelings about war in general, and my whole approach to survival had become mixed up. Fortunately, at that time it was announced that we would be sent away from the front lines to Southern France where we would regroup and trained to handle the release of prisoners of war in the concentration camps. I had spent about as many days on the front as I was able to handle and was indeed relieved.

I was transferred to another squad as assistant squad leader. A staff sergeant had come along and took my place as the head of my hillbilly group. At best leading them had been an exercise in futility as far as I was concerned. More and more I had sunk into a depression. It looked like this was never going to end.

I was then hit by shrapnel, but it was just a glancing blow off my right shoulder. It knocked me to the ground. It was not enough to report but that was the only time I was actually hit during my stay at the front.

The orders came through to replace us on the front. We were to be prepared for the special assignment.

Without incident, we were trucked back to the Southern part of France. The first day we were there I was required to take troops out and instruct them on the use of the M-1 rifle. The date was April 15, 1945. I took the squad far out into the field, over a hill into a private area where we wouldn't be disturbed. We went over all of the intricacies of the rifle and its usage as well as safety features.

In the course of closing the short course, I squatted to talk to them. There was a large pop and my knee locked under me. It was the most intense and unbelievable pain I had experienced until that time. I could not even touch the toe of my foot to the ground without terrible shooting pains going up into my groin. The medics were called and it was determined that they would have to evacuate me. Because we were on the side of this hill they couldn't get an ambulance up to me so I had to be carried about a block or two down to the ambulance.

The pain was indeed intense. I can't report much about time lapse or events. I do know that it came as a real shock and almost an insult to my youthful ego to have to be carried away for a trivial injury such as this, after all I had gone through. I had failed. Despondency was well upon me at that time. It indeed looked like a rather dismal conclusion to my sincere effort and desire to do an exceptionally good job. As the medic people were putting me on the stretcher I looked back up the hill. All of a sudden large numbers of people were running down the hill toward us. These were not just people from our company but a number from other companies. I don't really know how they got the word in that short period of time or where they all came from, but they were all there when they picked me up, and placed me on a stretcher to make my descent and exit. These were people I had had significant contacts with over the past few months. In a sense it was dramatic because even though they were only dirty old infantry men, they at least represented my honor guard as I left. I think there were good wishes and everything as they kind of lined up on both sides of the pathway, but I was almost oblivious to what was happening. As we got to the end of the line I heard this gruff whisper "there goes the best damn Sergeant in the United States Army." It didn't have much impact on me at the time but later lying in the hospital in Rennes, France, I thought much about it. Well, what do you know, I must have touched a few along the way. Believe me, in my nineteen year old heart, that meant a great deal.

When the stretcher bearers got to the ambulance and lifted me in, although I couldn't move, I could look back. Much to my surprise all of the officers were standing on the top of the hill. The enlisted men were immobile along the pathway. They hadn't moved. That was the last I saw or heard from any of them.

At that point a new life opened for me. I slammed shut the door to the room containing all of the pain, suffering, horror of it all, disappointment and fear. That door was re-opened several years ago when I started having strong feelings about relating what happened. My children had been after me for years to tell them about the war. It wasn't that so much, however, as a recognition that this story might be important to somebody someday and certainly contains lessons I had to learn.

I told the story to three persons, Fr. Claire Bourdereaux, my confessor, Fr. John Dietzen, my very close friend and Fr. Val Peter, a friend who had been involved closely with death and dying instances. Each insisted that the story be told in detail. This I attempt to do on these pages. It has been a very, very difficult task. Once the door was shut, I did not want to ever re-open it and fully intended that everything you have read would go with me to the grave. The dictating of this has been most traumatic. It has taken me three years to complete. I just couldn't get into it. Psychologically it was good for me to reopen the door and give you at least a few of the details of those months in France, Belgium and Germany. What had started as an ordinary part of life had turned into a most profound religious experience.

In writing this history, my thoughts go back to the initial conversations with the Lieutenant who was concerned that we weren't street fighters or tough enough. I was very young and cocky when I answered his concerns with a caustic "we'll do what we have to do -- no problem." It seemed so easy then, we did what we had to do. In those few months, I had passed from a boy to manhood and in all fairness, nothing along the way was quite as easy or as simple as I thought it would be.

Just before leaving the Company I had been unofficially informed by the Company Clerk that out of the 225 Complement of our Company on December 16, 1944, nine were left. Not a very good percentage. I didn't have the opportunity to check the accuracy of that statement.

Please, one should not interpret any of this adventure story as an attempt to exalt myself. Whatever happened in the way of heroism I can certainly attribute to the tremendous graces of our Almighty Father which were bestowed on me during those moments. I do not pretend to be a hero or anything unusual. I would be a fraud if I would leave that impression with anyone.

I have generally been unkind and critical of some Intelligence units. I am sorry about that, as I certainly hold no grudge against any man or group. I suppose we all did our very best under the circumstances. What the Hell! With all our faults our few divisions brought the elite of Hitler's corps to their knees. I really do know that Company B and the 106th Infantry Division officers, noncoms and men heroically did their duty against unbelievable odds. I believe all of us who survived could and did walk away with heads held high.

As to my out of body experience, history has recorded many unusual events and/or miracles which have taken place in the lives of people. Many times, if not most times, these miraculous happenings take place in the lives of the very least of the brothers and sisters in Christ. So it was in this instance.

EPILOGUE

You have read the story of a teenager written by one many years older but really transcribing events through the eyes, mentality and feelings of a teenager. I am now a grandfather and attempting to comment on those events and the events of this day from the perspective of a grandfather.

A good grandfather, will attempt to give love, advice, moral direction and evidence compassion for his grandchildren. He has nothing personally to gain other than the hope that they will listen to his comments on life and the lessons that he has learned, using same as stepping stones for their own future. There is nothing selfish in the advice of a good grandfather; just the feeling of need to communicate what has gone on before and hope the grandchildren will tie it into what is going on at the present time. If there is any teenager who wants to adopt a grandfather for the purpose of reading this -- feel free. It is written for all of you.

I am not personally responsible for your upbringing and only ask that you accept that this advice is given by one who has at least a scintilla of knowledge as to what is going on in this country today. The decisions and the adversities which we had to deal with during the war were tremendous. They dealt many times with life or death. Now, you all have come along and many things are happening to you. The dramatics involved in the war story are not necessarily involved in your life drama, but certainly the lessons which you will be learning or have learned create a tremendous responsibility and need for you to understand that <u>you and only you are responsible for your own actions and omissions</u>. Accept that challenge and you will immediately grow in spirituality and maturity.

It is true the players have changed a little bit since we were teenagers and the monsters of the past who would try to control the world have been replaced by new ogres. By act and dedication to violence, crime, fear, bullying and perversity the new monsters are no different from and probably just as horrible now as in the old days.

If you are a thinking and caring person you should have a sense and feeling even at this early age that your life is very special; that you are not an accident or fluke of the universe but you were specially created by a loving God. Never forget you have a purpose on earth which can only be fulfilled by your courage and focus.

The decisions which you face are on a continuing basis and if you are to do the right thing and during the turmoil and immorality of today become the person you should become, you have to make a commitment to excellence and goodness far beyond any such decisions made in combat.

I now understand that the "human condition" or "human situation", however you want to define it, permeates all other facets of life and has a universal impact on everyone, even though the actual traumas of life will differ with each person. This whole story is really about the human condition and life as it is and how we have to experience it. It is also about loving and caring for people you might never see again. You must give up all thoughts of self for the needs and caring for other people. The courage to embrace that priority is a condition precedent to your happiness and fulfillment as a person.

As part of my learning experience came the delayed realization that what over the years I considered to be a personal experience with our Creator, might not have been totally personal, might not have been totally private, but one which should have been shouted from the housetops.

It has been explained to me that we all have minor transfigurations in the course of our lifetimes if we remain close to the Lord. Perhaps yours has not yet happened or was not quite as dramatic as the one listed in the war story. However, if you think back certain events and certain things in your life occurred where you were swept away with great feelings of love and dedication for Our Lord Jesus Christ. These minor miracles which are treated by most as personal feelings are probably for the most part forgotten as life goes on; yet are part of the basketful of graces which Jesus holds available to each and every one of us who comes looking for help. Bishop Edward W. O'Rourke, retired Bishop of Peoria, Illinois aptly put it, as follows:

> We are "temples of God" where the Father, Son and Holy Spirit have "come to make their dwelling place." (John 14,

23) We carry within us the Holy Spirit, the ultimate source of the "glory" which shown through the body of Jesus when he was transfigured on Mount Tabor. Occasionally, our humdrum existence is replaced with a marvelous "spark" of the divine love within us. These experiences are awesome and also provide occasions for great acts of heroism. We might refer to them as "minor transfigurations."

We all still have to face death and my only prayer is that I can face it with the maturity I did as a growing boy. Death will come to each of us at such time as it is decreed by our God and the realization when it is imminent is going to be a shock to the system of each of us in varying degrees.

Each of us during our lifetime is subjected to adversities which make life tough and at times even unfair. These adversities come in varying degrees with different persons and families. We cope with them as best we can. With each adversity there is a tremendous lesson available for each to see and learn from. Adversities can be turned into positive possibilities but in every case the lessons are there for those who would learn. It is the wise man or woman who not only learns from hardship but who looks for the lesson in each case. Some of the key lessons I learned during the war are that life is much more important than just becoming king of the hill and acquiring possessions. We all have egos and for most of us in some way or another those egos grow out of control. We just have to overcome the feeling that our position, title, rank or how much we have in stocks, bonds, other assets or how many awards or personal triumphs we may have received have any importance at all; In the big picture those things just do not count. We all have to deal with self-centered persons so wrapped up in self and who can't worry about the problems of others. We have all had to cope with those persons who would attempt to control us, dominate our thoughts and actions, and use or manipulate us in order that they may acquire more power or riches. Avoid petty jealousies or being swept into this materialistic make believe existence.

We have to understand that we were not put in this world to sit in judgment of others or worry considerably about their transgressions. I have known and talked with people from all walks of life and suspect all of the above faults are temptations and problems which certainly touch the life of each of us.

Be kind and compassionate of others at all times and in every sense of the phrase. Temptations cannot be overcome until you learn that you were put on earth to serve others. All other needs will be met if you do your job to the best of your ability and focus on the care of those who come into your life and who desperately need help.

Learn to let go of any and all riches, possessions; power and control; and last of all, of any and all persons. They represent, if used intelligently, joys or pleasures which if put in proper prospective (and that's a big IF) can be used positively during your lifetime. These ties and "things" given their proper priorities, should never reign or control your life.

Remember the part of the war story where initially there was a lack of response from God; and then there was immediate response at such time as I could positively, and joyfully discard everything I had or was or wanted to be and voluntarily and again joyfully accept death if that would be His wish. At that moment a whole new series of events took charge in my life.

Think of our daily or almost daily saying of the Our Father and the phrase "thy will be done." That's easy to say in a common prayer. This becomes very difficult to say when the whole ballgame is on the line, especially if you have let other people and treasures of this world take over in your lifetime. If one can't learn to communicate with God daily with love and reverence, the necessary level of strength to cope with adversity cannot be reached.

It probably comes down to the question of priorities. No amount of attachments, no person or persons can affect your enjoyment and happiness if you have learned to discard them for a priority which we call the will of God -- "His will be done!"

If you believe in your heart that you were put on earth by a loving God who created you and made you for Himself; if you love Him and have followed His rules and commandments, it is my conviction that you will have bestowed on you more than ample graces to take care of the death situation when it comes along.

This does not mean that you have to reject life and envelop death each time you are sick. That is not consistent with rational behavior and our propensity to want to remain alive and preserve human life so long as it is the will of God.

It does mean that your priority is based on the fact that you are God's creature. You turn over to Him with joy and love the time, place and suffering necessary to successfully carry you into His presence and His kingdom.

Let's return for a moment to the events of 1944 and my immediate ecstasy, joy and the tremendous feelings of love and caring as explained in my discourse. This all happened to a teenager of 19 years who really hadn't thought about such events one way or another; and keep in mind we are discussing a close to death revelation which preceded most writings and modern communicated analysis on death by thirty or forty years.

What the hell did I know about death or this sort of thing? This joy and unbelievable happiness which was laid upon me had to come from somewhere. It certainly did not come from within. In fact, I was struck with absolute amazement. Could this have been a minor glimpse of what is in store for us when we cross over to the next segment of the eternal promises given by Jesus Christ? Of course it could!

The lessons for you to learn involve the same things that my generation went through. These teenage years are years when bodily changes are introduced to you and you have to be able to accept them physically as well as emotionally. It doesn't do me much good to preach to you about all the things that you have to learn. I am sure this has in many cases been done by your parents or by somebody along the way <u>ad nauseam</u>.

Let me just quickly go over a few things, however, and kind of check them off in your mind. You must keep your self-esteem and self-confidence.

It doesn't matter who else is involved, you have to believe in yourself. You have to be your own person and that your body is your temple and it is extremely stupid if you defile or destroy it.

You learned right from wrong in early days. Simply decide to do what is right and have the discipline and strength to follow through.

Be kind and charitable to all persons.

Pick and choose your companions very carefully.

Avoid all situations where you are not completely in control. Even though you are nice to everybody that doesn't mean you have to fraternize or be close to all people. Those that are bad will tear you down and destroy your morals. You can and will be dragged down to the gutter by a bad companion before you will ever be able to successfully rehabilitate that person. Rehabilitation should not be attempted by amateurs, but only those who have professional knowledge as to what is going on and what to do about it.

Avoid all those whom you neither like nor respect.

Have the courage and resolve to do the right thing at all times.

Understand peer pressure and what it means. We all want to be accepted. That doesn't end with teenage, but during the teenage years you have pressures and overwhelming feelings to be a part of the crowd and be accepted. What is right and wrong are sometime overlooked on the theory that "everybody is doing it."

Understand that you would not be normal if you did not resent authority and parental and societal restrictions at times. Understand these feelings for what they are because even though you are crying for independence, if you are honest with yourself you are also crying for somebody to help you take control.

What is the "in crowd" to you now won't be the "in crowd" in a couple of years and your life may go on a long, long time.

Most people are like sheep and will follow the direction of leaders without understanding where they are being led. March to your own drummer.

No matter what the odds may be when you know and feel sure you are doing the right thing and going in the right direction, do not deviate. You can rely on your conscience but only after you have been properly informed as to the moral equations involved in any given situation. This is where your family and religious upbringing can give you direction.

Never give up, never quit.

Avoid any occasions of sin or wrong and particularly stay away from sexual situations, bad companions, drugs and any persons who would lead you to physical or spiritual conduct which is unworthy of you and addictive once you give in.

Understand that you cannot accomplish these good and lofty aspirations all by yourself. God must come into your life. At such time as you open the door and communicate with him He will come in. If you don't invite him in, He will not force Himself on you. You must want with your whole heart to be in union with Him. You must make a commitment to Him. At that point He will enter your life and give you the courage and strength to do the right thing. You cannot do it by yourself, you can only do it by His help. When I refer to God, I of course, refer to Jesus Christ, who is one and the same with God the Father, together with the Holy Spirit.

Life can be an absolute ball if you keep your conscience clean and go down a road where you trust in God, don't tie yourself up with self-centeredness or selfishness but rather care about and concern yourself about the needs of other people. All the other things will fall into place.

Do not take yourself too seriously and at all times keep your sense of humor. Be sure to keep together with your family, no matter what, unless there are moral reasons which require you to avoid one or more of them.

As I moved forward in telling my story I hoped to include you in it by conveying some of the common challenges and problems in our lives. There were and are deep spiritual applications which have to be addressed.

It takes more courage to be a straight teenager now than it did in the 40's. If you are going to be something special, if you are going to change the world, you must have the courage to dream and work on those dreams. You have to be tenacious in making the dreams come true and these goals can't be accomplished without a continuing liaison with God.

If you lead your life in that manner and cling to those who believe as you do, a basketful of graces overflowing will take you through a wonderland of miracles that far exceed anything my poor human intellect can imagine or convey to you.

You are being called upon to be a hero, to be kind and generous and giving. You are asked to look at life in and with people who are in need. You are asked to keep the commandments of God. You have to know when to say yes and when to say no, and the courage to move upon that conviction.

Left to its own devices mankind will self-destruct. We humans are totally incapable of continuing goodness and unselfish love over a sustained period of time without the grace and love of God. We cannot enjoy that support if we don't follow the repeated demands of Jesus to love God and our fellow man.

History has recorded time after time the civilizations out of control and ultimately destroyed because of sin and perversity. History does repeat itself and it can certainly happen to our country. Even though America appears strong from the outside, we can decay internally if we are not morally straight, and we are far along the road of self-destruction at this time. The issues are becoming obvious. Have the courage to take a stand for what is right, regardless of the popularity of that stand at a given time.

For you this means that you simply have to ask whether what you have been taught about right and wrong, about family life, about God is a lie.

Jesus Christ is either God, your model and redeemer or the biggest liar the world has ever known. You are being lied to all right, and you have to determine who is telling the truth. You cannot respond to the admonitions of Christ and go along with this sinful world that we live in. Jesus said that if you deny Him you will also be denying the Father and if you deny the Father and the Son you reject all of Christianity. There is a high stakes live or die contest going on in America today. The prize is your soul. The tragedy is that many people are not even aware of this ongoing combat.

If you proclaim yourself as a Christian and go along with the church you will be subjected to ridicule, laughed at and persecuted. You must accept that. At the present time we have a media which is controlled by many persons who do not even believe in God but through devious means and bombardments on a continuing basis will put you in a position of having to defend your beliefs and the religious instruction of the centuries.

The goal and the essence of spiritual life is getting close to and moving toward union with Jesus and the Father. Therefore your religious affiliation is most important. It should be prayerfully and carefully chosen. It must keep you focused and provide stimulus to move you, in the long pull, toward that ultimate goal.

Give up any thoughts of instantaneous gratification and the "if it feels good do it" cult. The ultimate stupidity in this modern thrust is obvious -- but apparently dangerously successful in some younger circles.

Cults are going to come along from time to time and you should avoid them. Don't look for any church or religion of this world to be perfect. As long as they are guided by mortals there will be frailties and flaws to some extent. However, the Church as we know it has guided us and for over 2,000 years protected us from grave doctrinal mistakes. The structure, continuity and overall goodness of Christ's church has remained unbelievably strong and vibrant, certainly above and beyond other purely human institutions. You will recall Jesus himself said He would be with His Church until the end of the world.

If at the time this treatise comes into your hands you have made some very bad decisions or have had to undergo adverse circumstances in your life due to bad or sinful things which may have imposed upon you (or which you have imposed upon yourself) it does not mean that this wondrous world and this wondrous promise of happiness for all eternity cannot be yours.

If you have suffered illness or health problems in any way which tend to give you feelings of inferiority or lack of confidence you should also understand that there is still a <u>special</u> purpose for your life. You have to work out and fulfill that purpose in your own way, fighting through the physical or even mental distractions. God had a distinct purpose in creating you. There will never be another person like you and <u>I can't emphasize enough the</u>

importance of your keeping faith with yourself and believing in yourself

If you are living in sin or the victim of drugs or under the control of persons who are preying on you, by all means get help and divorce yourself from those people. You can be reborn into new life as a Christian which will allow all the joy and fulfillment that we have talked about.

****

I can yet vividly recall standing immobile and somewhat surrounded by the bodies of my dead friends. The day was November 18, 1944. The battle had just waned. The enemy had disbursed and the terrible shelling had stopped.

As I stood and endured that lonely vigil, I knew I could never again be the same person. These men had given their very lives for their country. They had been close friends. We had shared the closest of feelings and had mutual aspirations. For the most part they were virtually boys who believed in the goodness and justice of our crusade against tyranny. Most were small town boys and most had seen very little of the blessings and material things of this world. We had talked much about duty and responsibility. You will recall earlier on we discussed some of those conversations. Without questioning, these men fulfilled that duty under odds so slim that death seemed inevitable. Indeed inevitable it was for them.

They were and are my heroes. During all of our time together there was never a discussion of rights or that it was unfair that they might possibly die so early without a chance to live their lives out. At the end they had to make a decision against selfishness. They became givers. They rejected taking.

They could have fled under the stress of this horrible battle. Some others did flee. They could have cowered in their foxhole rather than be a part of the vanguard of the counter attack. Some others had stayed undercover. They chose to take the risk and lost their lives.

The world we all take for granted has been given to us on a platter by these heroes and the untold thousands like them. All of the opportunities which we have had and will have and the chance for liberty and a good life have been given to us as donees.

The lesson I learned from that battle is that I too had to become a giver and not a taker. As the years have gone on one finds very quickly who the givers and takers are. Givers are those who will fulfill their eternal destiny and purpose on this earth. Be one of them.

It is now time for your generation to become leaders of America and indeed the whole world. It is now your time to be heroes and heroines for all humanity. It is your time to forget yourself and think of others and like those soldiers I referred to, understand that this new generation has to limit wild and selfish demands as to individual rights unless and until you simultaneously embrace all duties that are concomitant to each and every one of those rights. The continuing price for preserving freedom and liberty will always remain high but it must be paid.

****

We have talked about many things in here, including those big words such as responsibilities, caring, loving, living, God, patriotism. You can find a good school or a good teacher to give you the fundamentals of reading, writing and arithmetic. However, in the things that really matter such as life, love, liberty, God and facing reality you have to experience life for yourself. I couldn't find the words to explain or communicate what had happened to me that one cold night. I still can't. This is true of anyone who has had a vision or who has faced incredible beauty or joy or any of these other aesthetics.

However, throughout your life these lessons will be made known to you just as they were showered upon me. It is your call as to whether you will accept those lessons and move onward and upward from there. I assure you in some manner or fashion and in a way entirely different and unique from the way that everybody else gets a shot at the lessons, you will be given the opportunity to see, progress to the extent you are capable. When your priorities are properly aligned, you will be able to understand and embrace the kingdom which has been set aside for you for all eternity. Don't blow it.

When you come to the happy and exciting realization that if you accept Jesus and submit yourself totally to His will, you will gain a new partner in life who will lead you to that ultimate goal of union with God. Remember the unbelievable miracles which fell upon me during the war. My new partner did that for me and He will do it for you. Even if the whole world is against you, your new partner will ultimately lead and carry you through to glory and joy forever. You will have surmounted all obstacles and won the battle despite all odds.

I've been very general in giving advice about lessons and directions. That has been deliberate. Have no fear. God will make the lessons obvious to you at such times as He deems proper -- if you just open that door.

With all my heart I believe and trust in the above statements. Always remember good Grandfathers (natural or adopted) don't lie.

DFV/p/war

6/21/94

ABOUT THE AUTHOR

Donald Francis Vonachen, known as "Bud", was born September 17, 1925 in Peoria, Illinois. He enlisted in the United States Army in 1943 at the age of 18. He served in the Battle of the Bulge with Company B, 424th Regiment, 106th Infantry Division, where he achieved the rank of Sergeant. For his valor in World War II, Bud was awarded the Bronze Star Medal. After the war, Bud returned home and married Patricia Clark in 1947. He attended Bradley University and the University of Wisconsin, and graduated with a Juris Doctor from the University of Illinois College of Law in 1950. In 1966 he coauthored *With Heart and Hand; a Guide to Personal Prayer for the Modern Catholic*, presented by the United States Department of the Army. Throughout his life he was incredibly active in Peoria area nonprofit organizations, but he always gave priority to his family and church. Bud remained a staunch Roman Catholic until his death at his home in Peoria on October 6th, 2005. He is survived by his wife Pat, his seven children, and their families.

Made in the USA
Monee, IL
15 March 2020